Preface

Numerical techniques form an integral part of computer science education, providing students with the tools to solve complex mathematical problems using algorithmic approaches. Understanding these techniques is essential for developing efficient, accurate, and logical problem-solving abilities. In recognition of their importance, the Indira Gandhi National Open University (IGNOU) has included this subject as a core component of the BCA curriculum, ensuring students build a solid foundation in computational mathematics.

"IGNOU BCA Computer Oriented Numerical Technique Previous Year Unsolved Papers BCS 054" has been carefully compiled to help students enhance their preparation through practice with real exam questions. This collection of previous years' unsolved question papers encourages independent thinking, sharpens analytical skills, and reinforces conceptual understanding. By working through these papers, learners can familiarize themselves with the exam format, identify key topics, and assess their readiness—making this book a practical and essential resource for academic success in BCS-054.

Table of Contents

BACHELOR OF COMPUTER APPLICATIONS (BCA) (REVISED)

Chapter 1: Term-End Examination, December- 2013

BCS-054: COMPUTER ORIENTED NUMERICAL TECHNIQUES

Time: 3 Hours
Maximum Marks: 100
Note: (i) Simple (but not scientific) calculator is allowed during the examination.
(ii) Question No. 1 is compulsory. Attempt any three from the next four questions.

1. (a) Using 8-decimal digit floating-point representation (4 digits for mantissa, 2 digits for exponent, and one each for sign of exponent and mantissa), represent the following numbers in normalized floating-point form:
(i) 89.36
(ii) –0.00004375
(iii) 87604 (use chopping, if required) 3

(b) Find the sum of two floating numbers:
$x_1 = .5307\times10^4$ and $x_2 = 0.4252\ \ 10^3$. 2

(c) Find the product of the two numbers in (b) above. 2

(d) What is underflow? Give an example of multiplication in which underflow occurs. 3

(e) Write the following system of linear equations in matrix form:
5x – 9y =14
2x + 5y = 11 2

(f) Solve the following system of linear equations using the Gauss elimination method:
3x + 4y =11
x + 3y = 7 3

(g) Find an interval in which the following equation has a root:
– 7x + 12 = 0 2

(h) Write the formula used in the Newton-Raphson method for finding the roots of an equation. 3

(i) Write the expressions obtained by applying each of the following operators to f(x), for some h:
(i) δ (ii) E (iii) μ 3

(j) Write Δ and δ in terms of E. 2

(k) State the following two formulas for interpolation:
(i) Newton's Forward difference formula
(ii) Stirling's formula 3

(l) Construct a difference table for the following data:

x	1	2	3	4
f(x)	2	9	28	65

2

(m) From the Newton's Forward difference formula asked in part k(i), derive the formula for finding the derivative of a function f(x) at . 3

(n) State the Trapezoidal rule for finding the integral (x) dx . 3

(o) Define each of the concepts with a suitable example:
(i) Degree and order of a differential equation
(ii) Initial Value Problem 4

2.(a) Briefly discuss how zero is represented as a floating-point number for the 8-decimal digit representation mentioned in Q. No. 1(a). 4

(b) For each of the following numbers, find the floating-point representation, if possible normalized, using rounding, if required. The format is 8-decimal digits as mentioned under Q. No. 1(a):

(i) 7854302

(ii) 2/3

Find absolute error, if any, in each case. 6

(c) Let $a = 476.9 \times 10^6$, $b = 657.2 \times 10^4$, and $c = -5.342 \times 10^4$. Find out whether '+' is associative for a, b, and c?

(i.e., you have to find out whether $(a + b) + c = a + (b + c)$ or not?) 10

BACHELOR OF COMPUTER APPLICATIONS (BCA) (REVISED)

Chapter 2: Term-End Examination, December- 2014

BCS-054: COMPUTER ORIENTED NUMERICAL TECHNIQUES

Time: 3 Hours
Maximum Marks:100
Note: (i) Simple (but not scientific) calculator is allowed during the examination.
(ii) Question No. 1 is compulsory. Attempt any three from the next four questions.

1.(a) Using 8-decimal digit floating-point representation (4 digits for mantissa, 2 for exponent, and one each for sign of exponent and mantissa), represent the following numbers in normalized floating point form (use rounding, if required):
(i) 9561
(ii) -74.794
(iii) -0.00726 3

(b) What is an overflow? Give an example involving the addition of numbers in which overflow occurs. 3

(c) Find the sum of two floating-point numbers: $x_1 = 0.4507\ \ 10^3$ and $x_2 = 0.5671\ 10^5$. 2

(d) Find the product of the two numbers given in question no. 1(c) above. 2

(e) Write the following system of linear equations in matrix form:
-8x + 6y =13
9x - 5y = 7 2

(f) Solve the following system of linear equations using the Gauss Elimination method:
4x + 3y = 1
7x - 2y = -20 3

(g) Find an interval in which the following equation has a root:
- 8x + 11 = 0 2

(h) Write the formula used in the Regula-Falsi method for finding the roots of an equation. 3

(i) Write the expressions obtained by applying each of the operators to f(x), for some h:
(i) Δ (ii) δ (iii) D 3

(j) Write each of V and δ in terms of E. 2

(k) State the following two formulas for interpolation:
(i) Newton's Backward difference formula
(ii) Stirling's formula 3

(l) Construct a difference table for the following data:

X	1	2	3	4
f(x)	2	5	10	17

2

(m) From Newton's Backward difference formula in part k(i), derive the formula for finding the derivative of a function f(x) at x_0 . 3

(n) State Simpson's (1/3) rule for finding the value of the integral $\int_a^b f(x)\,dx$. 3

(o) Explain each of the following concepts with a suitable example:
(i) Degree and order of a differential equation
(ii) Boundary Value Problem 4

2. (a) Can the number zero (0) be represented as a normalized floating-point number? Why or why not? Further, under the representation of question no. 1(a), how many floating-point representations (including all un-normalized representations) are possible for the number zero? 4

(b) For each of the following numbers, find the floating-point representation, if possible normalized, using rounding if required. The format is 8-digit as is mentioned in question no. 1(a):

(i) 2/7

(ii) 896786

Further, find the absolute error, if any, in each case. 6

(c) Find the product of the two numbers:

$a = -0.5203 \times 10^{4}$ and $b = -0.6251 \times 10^{-5}$ 6

(d) Find the approximate value of e by taking the first four terms of Maclaurin's series and also find the truncation error. 4

BACHELOR OF COMPUTER APPLICATIONS (BCA) (REVISED)

Chapter 3: Term-End Examination, June- 2015

BCS-054: COMPUTER ORIENTED NUMERICAL TECHNIQUES

Time: 3 Hours
Maximum Marks: 100
Note:(i) Simple (but not scientific) calculator is allowed during the examination.
(ii) Question No. 1 is compulsory. Attempt any three from the next four questions.

1.(a) Using an 8-decimal digit floating-point representation (4 digits for mantissa, 2 for exponent, and one each for sign of exponent and mantissa), represent the following numbers in normalized floating-point form (using chopping, if required):

(i) 8742 6
(ii) -94.2 7
(iii) -0.000346 3

(b) For the following two floating-point numbers:
$x_1 = 0.4527 \times 10^4$ and $x_2 = 0.5243 \times 10^3$, find $x_{1\_}x_2$. 2

(c) Find the product of x_1 and x_2 given in Q. No. 1(b) above. 2

(d) What is underflow? Explain it with an example of multiplication in which underflow occurs. 3

(e) Write the following system of linear equations in matrix form:
6x + 8y =10
-5x + 3y = 11 2

(f) Solve the system of linear equations given in Q. No. 1(e) above. 3

(g) Find an interval in which the following equation has a root:
$4x^2$ - 4x - 3 = 0 3

(h) Give one example of each of (i) algebraic equation (ii) transcendental equation. 2

(i) Write the expressions obtained by applying each of the operators to f(x), for some h:
(i) Δ $(ii)\nabla$ (iii)E (iv) δ 4

(j) Write and δ in terms of E. 2

(k) State the following two formulas for (equal interval) interpolation:
(i) Newton's Backward Difference Formula
(ii) Newton's Forward Difference Formula 3

(l) Construct a difference table for the following data:

x	1	2	3	4
f(x)	2	9	28	65

(m) From the Newton's Forward Difference Formula asked in Q. No. 1(k)(ii) above, derive the formula for finding derivative of a function at x_0 . 3

(n) State Simpson's (1/3) rule for finding the value of the integral $\int_a^b f(x)\,dx$. 3

(o) Explain each of the following concepts with a suitable example:
(i) Initial Value Problem
(ii) Degree and order of a differential equation 4

2.(a) Let min. and max. represent respectively minimum and maximum positive real numbers representable by some floating-point number system. Can every real number between max. and min. be representable by such a number system? Explain the reason for your answer. 4

(b) For each of the following numbers, find the floating-point representation, if possible normalized,

using chopping, if required. The format is 8-digit as is mentioned in Q. No. 1(a):

(i) 3/11

(ii) 74.0365

Further, find the absolute error, if any, in each case. 6

(c) Find a ÷ b (a divided by b) for the floating point numbers:

$a = - 0.4783 \times 10^4$; $b = 0.5237 \times 10^{-5}$ 6

(d) Find the Taylor's series for \frac{1}{x} at a = 1. 4

BACHELOR OF COMPUTER APPLICATIONS (BCA) (REVISED)

Chapter 4: Term-End Examination, December- 2015

BCS-054: COMPUTER ORIENTED NUMERICAL TECHNIQUES

Time: 3 Hours
Maximum Marks: 100
Note: 1. Simple (but not scientific) calculators are allowed.
2. Question number 1 is compulsory. Attempt any three from the next four questions.

1. (a) Explain, with suitable examples, the advantages of using normalized form for representing numbers. 3

(b) Using 8-decimal digit floating point representation (with four digits for mantissa, two for exponent, and one each for sign of exponent and mantissa), represent the following numbers in normalized floating point form
(use chopping if required):
(i) 8975
(ii) — 897.87
(iii) — 0.0078456 4

(c) For two floating point numbers x_1=0.6187×10^4 and x_2=0.5306×10^3, find $x_1 - x_2$ in floating point representation. 2

(d) Find the product of the two numbers given in question number 1(c) above 2

(e) Write the following system of linear equations in matrix form:
7x−5y=9 x
−8x−4y=−13 2

(f) Show one iteration of solving the following system of linear equations using any iterative method. Assume x=y=0 as the initial estimate:
−8x+7y= 15
5x−2y=−7 3

(g) Find an interval in which the following equation has a root:
−5x+6=0 2

(h) Write the formula used in Newton-Raphson method for finding the root of an equation. 3

(i) Write the three expressions obtained by applying the operators to f(x) for some h:
(i) ∇ $(ii) E$ $(iii) D$ 3

(j) Write each of Δ and μ in terms of E. 2

(k) State the following two formulas for interpolation:
i. Newton's Forward difference formula
ii. Stirling's formula 3

(l) Construct a difference table for the following data

X	1	2	3	4
f(x)	2	5	10	17

2

(m) Using Newton's Forward difference formula, derive the formula for finding the derivative of a function f(x) at . 3

(n) State the Trapezoidal rule for finding the value of the integral ∫(x) dx. 3

(o) Explain the following concepts with a suitable example:
i. Boundary Value Problem

ii. Order of a differential equation 4

2. (a) For each of the three numbers from question 1(b), find the relative error in its normalized floating point representation. 6

(b) Find the approximate value of e by taking the first three terms of the Maclaurin series and also find the truncation error. 4

(c) Solve the following system of linear equations using Gaussian elimination method and comment on the nature of the solution:

$$12x_1+18x_2-5x_3=25$$
$$3x_1-5x_2+7x_3=5$$
$$9x_1+23x_2-12x_3=20$$
5

(d) Obtain the smallest positive root of the equation $x^3-5x+1=0$, by using three iterations of the bisection method. 5

3.(a) Solve the following system of linear equations using Gaussian elimination with partial pivoting:

$$x_1-x_2+3x_3=3$$
$$2x_1+x_2+4x_3=7$$
$$3x_1+5x_2-2x_3=6$$
12

(b) Give the formula for the next approximation of x_1,x_2 *and* x_3 using Gauss-Seidel method for solving the system of linear equations:

$$a_{11}x_1 + a_{12}x_2 + a_{13}x_3 = b_1 \;;$$
$$a_{21}x_1 + a_{22}x_2 + a_{23}x_3 = 2 \;; \text{ and}$$
$$a_{31}x_1 + a_{32}x_2 + a_{33}x_3 = b_3$$
4

(c) Describe the relative merits of direct methods and iterative methods for solving systems of linear equations. 4

4. (a) The population of a city in a census taken once every 10 years is given below in thousands. Estimate the population in 1965 8

Year	**1961**	**1971**	**1981**	**1991**	**2001**	**2011**
Population (in 000s)	35	42	58	84	120	165

(b) Derive the operators E and Δ in terms of δ. 5

(c) Find Newton's backward difference form of the interpolating polynomial for the following Data 7

x	**4**	**6**	**8**	**10**
f(x)	19	40	83	155

Hence evaluate f(9):

5. Attempt any **two** of the following:

(a) Find the approximate value of the integral I=$\int_1^3 \frac{dx}{4+3^x}$using Simpson's $\left(\frac{1}{3}\right)$ rule (three points).

10

(b) The values of y= $\sqrt{x}$ are given below for x=1.5,(0.5),3.5

X	1.5	2.0	2.5	3.0	3.5
f(x)	1.2247	1.4142	1.5811	1.7320	1.8708

Find y′ and y″ at x=3.25 using the BD formula:

(c) Solve the following initial value problem using Euler's method:
y′=1 − 2xy, y(0.2)=0.1948, find y(0.4) h= 0.2. 10

BACHELOR OF COMPUTER APPLICATIONS (BCA) (REVISED)

Chapter 5: Term-End Examination, June- 2016

BCS-054: COMPUTER ORIENTED NUMERICAL TECHNIQUES

Time: 3 Hours
Maximum Marks: 100
Note: 1. Simple (but not scientific) calculators are allowed.
2. Question number 1 is compulsory. Attempt any three from the next four questions.

1. (a) Explain, the concept (i) Chopping, (ii) rounding ,each with a suitable example. 3

(b) Using 8-decimal digit floating point representation (with four digits for mantissa, two for exponent, and one each for sign of exponent and mantissa), represent the following numbers in normalized floating point form (use chopping if required):
(i) 8975
(ii) — 897.87
(iii) — 0.0078456 4

(c) For two floating point numbers $x_1 = 0.7108 \times 10^5$ and $x_2 = 0.8701 \times 10^4$ find $x_1 + x_2$. 2

(d) Find the product of the two numbers given in question number 1(c) above. 2

(e) Write the following system of linear equations in matrix form:
-9x−5y= -4
3x+4y=−17 2

(f) Show one iteration of solving the following system of linear equations using any iterative method. Assume x=y=0 as the initial estimate:
−6x+8y= -4
3x+4y=−1 3

(g) Find an interval in which the following equation has a root:
x^2+9x+20=0 2

(h) Write the formula used in Secant method for finding the root of an equation. 3

(i) Write the three expressions obtained by applying the operators to f(x) for some h:
(i) E $(ii)\ \Delta$ $(iii)\ \nabla$ 3

(j) Write each of ∇ and δ in terms of E. 2

(k) State the following two formulas for interpolation:
(i) Newton's Backward difference formula
(ii) Bessel's formula 3

(l) Construct a difference table for the following data 2

X	4	5	6	7
f(x)	13	22	33	46

(m) Using Newton's Forward difference formula, derive the formula for finding the derivative of a function at x = x_0. 3

(n) State the Simpon's $\frac{1}{3}$ rule for finding the value of $\int_z^b f$(x) dx. 3

(o) Explain the following concepts with a suitable example:
(i) Order of a differential equation
(ii) Initial Value Problem

(iii) Degree of a differential equation

(iv) Non-linear differential equation 4

2. (a) For each of the three numbers from question 1(b), find the relative error in its normalized floating point representation. 6

(b) Using Maclaurin's series expansion, find the value of (1 - x) -1, at x = 0, by taking the first three terms and find truncation error. 4

(c) Attempt to solve the following system of linear equations using the Gauss elimination method

3x1 + 2x2 + x3 = 3

2x1 +x2 +x3 =0

6x1 + 2x2 + 4x3 = 6

Does the solution exist? If yes, how many? 5

(d) Starting with xo = 0, perform two iterations to find an approximate root of the equation x3 -4x + 1 = 0, using Newton-Raphson method. 5

3.(a) We have the following system of linear equations using Gaussian elimination method with partial pivoting condensation:

$3x_2 + 4x_3 = 2$

$4x_1 — 2x_2 + x_3 = 18$

$3x_1 + 4x_2 + 5x_3 = 11$

Compute upto two decimals only 12

(b) Give the formula for next approximation of values of x1, x2 and x3 using Gauss-Jacobi iterative method for solving the following system of linear equations:

$a_{11}x_1 + a_{12}x_2 + a_{13}x_3 = b_1$;

$a_{21}x_1 + a_{22}x_2 + a_{23}x_3 = b_2$;

$a_{31}x_1 + a_{32}x_2 + a_{33}x_3 = b_3$ 4

(c) Describe the relative merits and demerits of direct methods and iterative methods for solving systems of linear equations. 4

4. (a) Construct a difference table for the following data and mark the forward differences by underlying the numbers:

x	1	2	3	4	5	6	7	8
y	7	13	18	25	35	48	62	78

8

(b) Derive the operators δ and Δ in terms of E. 5

(c) Find Newton's backward difference form of the interpolating polynomial for the following data, and use it to evaluate f(12): 7

X	3	5	7	19	11	13
f(x)	16	36	64	100	144	196

5. Attempt any **two** of the following:

(a) Find the approximate value of the integral I=$\int_0^1 \frac{dx}{2+3x}$ using Simpson's $\frac{1}{3}$ rule (three points). 10

(b) The values of $y = \sqrt{x}$are given below for x=1.5,(0.5),3.5. 10

x	1.5	2.0	2.5	3.0	3.5
f(x)	1.2247	1.4142	1.5811	1.7320	1.8708

Find y' and y'' at x=3.25 using the backward difference formula:

(c) Solve the following initial value problem using Euler's method: $y' = f(t,y) + 1+y$; given $y(0) = 1$ find the solution on [0,0.8] with h=0.2. 10

BACHELOR OF COMPUTER APPLICATIONS (BCA) (REVISED)

Chapter 6: Term-End Examination, December- 2016

BCS-054: COMPUTER ORIENTED NUMERICAL TECHNIQUES

Time: 3 Hours
Maximum Marks: 100
Note: 1.Calculators, including scientific calculators, are allowed. However, each step of numerical calculation should be explicitly carried out by the examinee.
2.Question No. 1 is compulsory. Attempt any three questions from the remaining four.

1. (a) Find the sum of the two floating point numbers: a=0.5403×103 and b=0.7182×104. 3
(b) Find the product of the two numbers a and b given above. 3
(c) Define what is 'underflow'. Give an example of multiplication that results in underflow. 4
(d) Write the following system of linear equations in matrix form:
8x+11y=19
12x+5y=17 3
(e) Solve the following system of linear equations using the Gauss elimination method:
5x−3y=7
−2x+9y=5 4
(f) Find an interval in which the following equation has a root:
x^2+x−2=0 3
(g) Write briefly the steps of the bisection method to find the root of an equation. 4
(h) Write the expressions obtained by applying each of the following operators to f(x):
(i) δ
(ii) ∇ 4
(i) Write E in terms of each of Δ and separately. 3
(j) Construct the difference table for the following data. 3

x	1	5	9	13
f(x)	5	17	29	41

(k) State the following two formulas for interpolation (for equal intervals):
(i) Newton Forward Difference Formula
(ii) Bessel's Formula 3
(l) Explain the concept of an 'Initial Value Problem' with an example. 3

2. (a) Solve the following system of linear equations using partial pivoting:
$4x_1$-$5x_2$+$6x_3$=24
x_1+ $3x_2$ -$5x_3$ = 22
-$2x_1$ + $8x_2$ + x_3 = 11 10
(b) What are the relative advantages of iterative methods over direct methods for solving a system of linear equations? 5

3.(a) For f(x) = 3x3+11x−5, find ∇^3 f(x) in terms of h, where h is an equally spaced interval. 8

(b) Estimate the missing term in the following data using backward difference, assuming that the data represents a valid polynomial of degree 3: 12

X	1.20	1.40	1.60	1.80	2.00
f(x)	3.3201	4.0552	4.9530	?	7.3891

4.Attempt any **two** of the following:

(a) Find f'(x) at x=0.25 from the following table of values 10

X	0.2	0.3	0.4	0.5	0.6
f(x)	2.1082	2.8706	3.4013	3.9121	4.3012

(b) Find the approximate value of the integral $\int_2^3 \frac{dx}{3+4x}$ using the Trapezoidal rule, with 5 equal parts of [2, 3]. 10

(c) Using Euler's method to find the solution of dy/dx = 3x + y, given y(0) = 3, find the solution on the interval [0, 0.8] with h = 0.2, where x is the independent variable and y is the dependent variable. 10

5.(a) Using the 8-decimal digit floating point representation (4 digits for mantissa, 2 digits for exponent, and one each for sign of exponent and mantissa), represent the following numbers in normalized floating-point form:

(i) −98.37

(ii) 0.000893

(use chopping if required) 4

(b) Using the 8-decimal digit format stated in Q5(a) above, briefly discuss how zero is represented as a floating point number. 6

(c) Let a = 476.9 x 10^6, b = 657.2 x 10^4 and c = — 5.342 x 10^4. Find out whether `+' is associative for a, b and c (i.e., you are required to find out whether (a+b)+c=a+(b+c)or not) **10**

BACHELOR OF COMPUTER APPLICATIONS (BCA) (REVISED)

Chapter 7: Term-End Examination, June- 2017

BCS-054: COMPUTER ORIENTED NUMERICAL TECHNIQUES

Time: 3 Hours
Maximum Marks: 100
Note: 1.Calculators, including scientific calculators, are allowed. However, each step of numerical calculation should be explicitly carried out by the examinee.
2.Question No. 1 is compulsory. Attempt any three questions from the remaining four.

1. (a) Calculate x−y for the following two floating-point numbers:
$x=0.8706\times10^{-3}$, $y=0.7604\times10^{-2}$. 3
(b) Find the product of xxx and yyy given in (a) above. 3
(c) Explain what 'overflow' is, with a suitable example of multiplication. 4
(d) Write the following system of linear equations in matrix form:
$-9x+17y=-8$
$12x=23$
(e) Solve the following system of linear equations using the Gauss elimination method:
$-7x+5y=3$
$2x-8y=-12$
(f) Find an interval in which the following equation has a root:
$2x^2+6x-7=0$
(g) Write briefly the steps of the Secant method to find the root of an equation. 4
(h) Write the expressions obtained by applying the following operators to f(x):
(i)∇
(ii)Δ **4**
(i) Write Δ in terms of each of (i) E and (ii) δ separately.
(j) Construct the difference table for the following data:

x	2	7	11	17	23
f(x)	17	32	49	73	143

(k) State the following two formulas for interpolation (for equal intervals):
(i) Stirling's Formula
(ii) Newton's Backward Difference Formula
(l) Explain the concepts of 'order' and 'degree' of a differential equation, with an example. 2

2. (a) Using either the Gauss-Jacobi iterative method or the Gauss elimination method with partial pivoting, solve the following system of linear equations:
$3x-5y+6z=11$
$5x-11z=-28$
$2y+9z=31$ 15
(b) Discuss the merits and demerits of the direct approach over the iterative approach for solving a system of linear equations. 5

3.(a) For f(x)=4x3−3x2+8 find Δ^3 f(x) in terms of h, where h is an equally spaced interval. 8

(b) Estimate the missing term in the following data using the Forward Difference (FD) method, assuming the data is a valid representation of a polynomial of degree 3.

x	1.00	1.20	1.40	1.60	1.80
f(x)	2.7183	?	4.0552	4.9530	6.049

Attempt any **two** of the following:

4.(a) Approximate the value of $\int_3^4 \frac{dx}{4-3x}$ using the Trapezoidal rule, with five equal parts of the interval [3, 4] .10

(b) Using Euler's method, tabulate the solution of the Initial Value Problem (IVP) $y' = -3ty^2$, y(0) = 1 in the interval [0, 1], using h=0.2. 10

(c) From the data given in the table below, find $y' = \frac{dy}{dx}$ at x =2.75 using the Forward Difference method:

x	1.5	2.0	2.5	3.0	3.5
y= f(x)	1.2247	1.4142	1.5811	1.7320	1.8708

5.(a) Using the 8-decimal digit floating-point representation (4 digits for mantissa, 2 digits for exponent, and one each for sign of exponent and mantissa), represent the following numbers (use chopping if required):

(i)−76.384

(ii)0.00079542 **4**

(b) Is '+' associative when $a=0.2134\times10^5$;$b=0.2354\times10^3$;, and $c=-0.2142\times 10^1$ are three floating-point numbers to be added in this order? You are required to find whether (a+b) + c = a + (b+c). 10

(c) Explain the following two concepts with suitable examples:

(i) Chopping error

(ii) Rounding error 6

BACHELOR OF COMPUTER APPLICATIONS (BCA) (REVISED)

Chapter 8: Term-End Examination, December- 2017

BCS-054: COMPUTER ORIENTED NUMERICAL TECHNIQUES

Time: 3 Hours
Maximum Marks: 100
Note: 1. Any calculator is allowed during the examination.
2. Question No. 1 is compulsory. Attempt any three questions from the next four.

1. (a) Find the sum of two floating-point numbers:
x_1=0.4325×10^2 and x_2=0.3507×10^3. 2

(b) Find the product of x_1 and x_2 given in (a). 2

(c) Explain what 'Overflow' is. Give an example of multiplication due to which overflow occurs. 3

(d) Write the following system of linear equations in matrix form:
−8x+7y=15
12x−8y=4 **2**

(e) Solve the following system of linear equations using the Gauss elimination method:
5x−3y=7
−7x+15y=1 **4**

(f) Find an interval in which the following equation has a root:
x^2−9x+19=0 2

(g) Write the formula of the Newton-Raphson method for finding the root of an equation. 3

(h) Write the expressions obtained by applying the following operators:
(i)∇
(ii)δ
(iii) Δ 3

(i) Write ∇ and δ in terms of E. 3

(j) State the following two formulas for interpolation:
(i) Bessel's Formula
(ii) Newton's Forward Difference Formula 4

(k) Construct a difference table for the following data:

X	1	4	7	10
f(x)	6	10	14	18

(l) From the Newton's Forward difference formula asked in j(ii), derive a rule/formula for finding the derivative of a function f(x) at x= x_Q. 3

(m) State the Trapezoidal rule for finding the value of the integral $\int_a^b f(x)\,dx$. 3

(n) Define each of the following concepts with one suitable example:
(i) Differential Equation
(ii) Initial Value Problem 4

2.(a) Using 8-decimal digit floating point representation (with four digits for mantissa, two digits for exponent, and one each for the sign of exponent and mantissa), represent the following numbers in normalized floating point form (use chopping if required):

(i)8795

(ii)-798.78

(iii)-0.0087456 **3**

(b) For each of the three numbers in question 2(a), find the relative error in its normalized floating point representation. 6

(c) Find the approximate value of eee by taking the first three terms of Maclaurin's series and also find the truncation error. 3

(d) Obtain the smallest positive root of the equation x^3−5x+1=0, by using three iterations of the bisection method. 6

3.(a) Discuss the relative merits and demerits of each of the following for solving a system of linear equations:

(i) Direct methods

(ii) Iterative methods 4

(b) Solve the following system of linear equations using the Gaussian elimination method, and comment on the nature of the solution:

12x+18y−5z=25

3x−5y+7z=5

9x+23y−12z=20 6

(c) Solve the following system of linear equations with partial pivoting using the Gaussian elimination method:

x−y+3z=3

2x+y+4z=7

3x+5y−2z=6 10

4. (a) For f(x)=6+8x+9, find $\Delta 3\Delta^3$f(x). 6

(b) Estimate the missing term in the following data using the Forward Difference method:

x	100	101	102	103	104
log x	2.000	2.0043	?	2.0128	2.0170

(c) Derive the operators E and Δ in terms of δ. 6

Attempt any **two** of the following:

5. (a) Find the approximate value of $\int_2^3 \frac{dx}{1+x}$ using the Trapezoidal rule with h=0.25. 10

(b) Find f'(x) at x=0.1 from the following table of values:

x	0.2	0.3	0.4	0.5	0.6
f(x)	1.2214	1.3498	1.4918	2.56	3.02

(c) Using Euler's method, find the solution of the differential equation y'=t+y given y(0)=1, in the interval [0, 0.8] with step size h=0.2. The independent variable is t. 10

BACHELOR OF COMPUTER APPLICATIONS (BCA) (REVISED)

Chapter 9: Term-End Examination, June- 2018

BCS-054: COMPUTER ORIENTED NUMERICAL TECHNIQUES

Time: 3 Hours
Maximum Marks: 100
Note: 1. Any calculator is allowed during the examination.
2. Question No. 1 is compulsory. Attempt any three from the next four questions.

1.(a) Explain, with a suitable example, the advantages of using the normalized form for representing numbers. 3

(b) For two floating point numbers x_1=0.7268×10^5 and x_2=0.6271×10^4 find x_1-x_2 in floating point representation. 3

(c) Find the product of the two numbers given in question 1(b) above in floating point notation. 2

(d) Write the following system of linear equations in matrix form:

−8x+15y=−1
7x−4y=10 3

(e) Find an interval in which the following equation has a root:

x^2−12x+30=0. 2

(f) Write briefly the steps of the bisection method to find the roots of an equation. 3

(g) Write E and μ in terms of ∇. 2

(h) Write the expressions obtained by applying each of the following operators to f(x) for some h>0:

(i)D
(ii)E
(iii)∇ **3**

(i) State the formulas for the following interpolations:

(i) Newton's Forward Difference Formula
(ii) Stirling's Formula 4

(j) Construct a difference table for the following data:

X	1	2	3	4
f(x)	8	12	17	25

(k) State the Trapezoidal rule for finding the value of the integral $\int_a^b f(x)dx$. 3

(l) Explain each of the following concepts with a suitable example:

(i) Boundary value problem
(ii) Order of a differential equation
(iii) Degree of a differential equation 6

2.(a) Using 8-decimal digit floating point representation (with 4 digits for mantissa, 2 for exponent, and one each for the signs of mantissa and exponent), represent the following numbers in normalized floating point form:

(i)0.000725
(ii)−89.6532
(iii)−98876 **3**

(b) Briefly discuss how zero is represented as a floating point number in the 8-decimal digit representation mentioned in question 2(a). 4

(c) Let a=476.9×10^6, b=657.2×10^4, and c=−5.342×10^4. Find whether '+' is associative for a, b, and c (i.e., find whether a+(b+c)=(a+b)+c using the 8-decimal digit representation mentioned in question 2(a). 14

3.(a) Solve the following system of linear equations using Partial Pivoting:

2x−3y+5z=4
x+5y−4z=2
4x+3y−7z=0 11

(b) Explain the relative advantages of direct methods over iterative methods for solving a system of linear equations. 4

(c) Solve the following system of linear equations using the Gaussian Elimination Method:

8x−5y=11
3x+7y=13 5

4.(a) The population of a city in a census taken once in 10 years is given below in thousands. Estimate the value in 1975:

Year	1970	1980	1990	2000	2010
Population	45	52	68	94	130

(b) Derive the operators δ and Δ in terms of E. 5

(c) Find Newton's Backward Difference Form of the interpolating polynomial for the following data:

x	f(x)
6	21
8	42
10	85
12	157

Attempt any **two** of the following:

5. (a) Find the approximate value of the integral I=$\int_2^4 \frac{dx}{4+3^x}$ using Simpson's $(1/3)$ rule with h=0.5. 10

(b) The values of y = $\sqrt{x}$ are given below for x=1.5,(0.5)3.5. Compute the value of f'(x) at x=1.0:

X	1.5	2.0	2.5	3.0	3.5
f(x)	1.2247	1.4142	1.5811	1.7320	1.8708

(c) Solve the following Initial Value Problem (IVP) using Euler's method:

y'=1−2xy, y(0.2)=0.1948 Find y(0.4) with h=0.1. 10

BACHELOR OF COMPUTER APPLICATIONS (BCA) (REVISED)

Chapter 10: Term-End Examination, December- 2018

BCS-054: COMPUTER ORIENTED NUMERICAL TECHNIQUES

Time: 3 Hours
Maximum Marks:100
Note: 1. Use of calculator is allowed during the examination.
2. Question No. 1 is compulsory. Attempt any three questions from Questions No. 2 to 5.

1.(a) Assume that a floating point representation is of eight decimal digits with four digits for mantissa, two digits for exponent, and one digit each for the sign of exponent and mantissa. Answer the following using this representation (the numbers should be represented in normalized floating point form. Use chopping if required). Represent:

(i)−235
(ii)−2576
(iii)+0.007567 **3**

(b) What are the advantages of representing floating point numbers in normalized form? 2

(c) If x_1=2.98×10^2 and x_2=1.97×10^1 are two floating point numbers, find the value of $x_1 - x_2$. You must show all the steps. 2

(d) If x_3=2.71×10^4 and x_4=−1.53×10^{-5} are two floating point numbers, find the value of $x_3 \times x_4$. Show all the steps. 2

(e) Write the following system of linear equations in matrix form:

2x+y+z=5
x+3z=9
2y+5z=11 2

(f) Show one iteration of solving the following system of linear equations using the Gauss-Jacobi iterative method. You may assume x=1 and y=1 as the initial estimates:

2x+3y=8
3x+5y=13 3

(g) Find an interval in which the following equation has a root:

$4x^2$+4x−35=0 2

(h) Explain how the calculation of the next estimate differs in the Newton-Raphson method compared to the Bisection method of solving non-linear equations. 3

(i) Write the symbol and formula with respect to f(x)and some value of h for the following operators:

(i) Forward difference
(ii) Central difference
(iii) Shift operator 3

(j) Express the forward difference and backward difference operators in terms of the shift operator. 2

(k) State Newton's Forward Difference Formula for interpolation. 2

(l) Given the following data:

x	0	2	10	30
y	5	10	40	70

To find the value of y at x=5, which method would you choose: Lagrange's method or Newton's Backward Difference Formula? Give a reason in support of your answer. 2

(m) From the Forward Difference Formula for interpolation asked in question 1(k), derive the formula for finding the derivative of a function f(x) at x=x_0. 3

(n) State and explain the Trapezoidal rule geometrically. 4

(o) Define the following terms in the context of differential equations:

(i) Order
(ii)Degree
(iii)Initial condition
(iv)Boundary condition 4

2. (a) Explain the following terms with the help of an example:

(i) Truncation error
(ii) Absolute error
(iii) Overflow
(iv)Unstable problem 8

(b) Obtain the smallest positive root of the equation x^3−x−3=0, using three iterations of the Bisection method. 6

(c) What is Maclaurin's series? Find the Maclaurin series of f(x)=around x = 0. 6

3. (a) Solve the following system of linear equations using the Gaussian Elimination method with partial pivoting condensation:

x−2y+z=1
3x+y+3z=10
2x+3y−5z=2 10

(b) Using the Gauss-Seidel iterative method, show two iterations of solving the following system of linear equations:

$4x_1-x_2+x_3=10$
$2x_1+3x_2-x_3=4$
$x_1+2x_2+x_3=7$

Take initial estimates as x1=x2=x3=0. 6

(c) Which of the two methods, direct or iterative, would you choose for the following types of problems? Give reasons in support of your answer:

(i) When the matrix is dense and the order of the matrix is less than 50.
(ii) When you want small rounding off errors. 4

4. (a) Estimate the missing term (shown by "?") in the following data, if it represents a valid interpolating polynomial of degree 3:

X	2	3	4	5	6
f(x)	3	7	?	21	31

Also, find the interpolating polynomial using Newton's Forward Difference Formula and find the value of f(x) at x=2.5. 10

(b) Find Newton's Backward Difference Form of interpolating polynomial for the following data:

x	2	4	6	8
f(x)	21	41	80	140

Hence, evaluate f(7). 6

(c) Find f(x) and f(x) for the square function f(x)= x^2. 4

Attempt any **two** of the following:

5. (a) The values of y=$x^{3/2}$ are given for x=1.0,(0.5),3.0:

X	1.0	1.5	2.0	2.5	3.0
y= $x^{3/2}$	1.00	1.84	2.83	3.95	5.20

Find y′ and y″ at x=1.25 using the Forward Difference Formula. 10

(b) Evaluate $\int_1^6 (2 + x^2)\, dx$ using Simpson's rule with 11 points. 10

(c) Using Euler's method, find the solution of the differential equation y′=t^2+y ,
Given y(0)=1. Find the solution in the interval [0,0.8] with h=0.2. 10

BACHELOR OF COMPUTER APPLICATIONS (BCA) (REVISED)

Chapter 11: Term-End Examination, June- 2019

BCS-054: COMPUTER ORIENTED NUMERICAL TECHNIQUES

Time: 3 Hours
Maximum Marks: 100
Note:1. Use of calculator is allowed during the examination.
2. Question No. 1 is compulsory. Attempt any three questions from Questions No. 2 to 5.

1. (a) Find the sum of two floating-point numbers:
$x=0.6239\times10^6$ and $y=0.5163\times10^4$. 2

(b) Find the product of xxx and yyy where the values of xxx and yyy are given in part (a). 2

(c) What is "underflow"? Give an example of multiplication that leads to underflow. 3

(d) Write the following system of linear equations in matrix form:
$3x+5y+8z=0$
$3y+2z=7$
$2x-3z=-6$ 2

(e) Solve the following system of linear equations using the Gauss elimination method:
$13x-7y=2$
$5x+3y=15$ 4

(f) Find an interval in which the following equation has a root:
$2x^2-11x+14=0$ 2

(g) Show two iterations of the Newton-Raphson method for finding the approximate root of the equation
$x^2+x-6=0$ starting with $x_0=1$. 3

(h) Write the notation and formula for the following operators:
(i) Central difference operator
(ii) Shift operator
(iii) Forward difference operator 3

(i) Write ∇ and δ in terms of E. 3

(j) Define the term "interpolation" with the help of an example. State Newton's Backward Difference Formula for interpolation. 4

(k) Construct a difference table for the following data:

X	4	6	8	10
f(x)	9	15	29	31

(l) From Newton's Backward Difference Formula asked in part (j), derive a formula for finding the derivative of a function f(x) at x_0. 3

(m) State the Trapezoidal rule for finding the approximate value of the integral $I=\int_a^b f(x)dx$. Also, show it geometrically. 3

(n) Define the following terms and give one example for each in the context of differential equations:
(i) Order
(ii)Degree

(iii) Initial conditions
(iv) Boundary conditions 4

2. (a) Assuming an 8-decimal digit floating-point representation (with 4 digits for mantissa, 2 digits for exponent, and one each for sign of mantissa and exponent), represent the following numbers in normalized floating point form (use chopping if required):

(i) 23563 255
(ii) −63.27 832
(iii) −0.0000235 6

(b) For each of the three numbers in Question 2(a), find the relative error in its normalized floating point representation. 6

(c) Obtain the approximate value of the smallest positive root of the equation

x^3+4x−12=0

using three iterations of the Bisection method. 6

(d) Find the Maclaurin series of f(x)=e^x around x=0. (Please note $\frac{d}{dx}e^x = e^x$) Calculate the approximate value of e using the first four terms of this series. 6

3. (a) Solve the following system of linear equations with pivotal condensation using the Gaussian Elimination Method:

2x+3y−z=11
x−5y+7z=0
3x−y−3z=4 10

(b) Solve the following system of linear equations using the Gauss-Jacobi iterative method. Perform only three iterations:

5x−7y+3z=15
x−5y−2z=4
3x+2y+z=2

Take initial estimates as x=0, y=0, and z=0. 6

(c) Define the following terms with the help of an example:

(i) Ill-conditioned problem
(ii) Rounding-off errors
(iii) Algebraic equations
(iv) Transcendental equations 4

4. (a) Find the Newton's Forward-Difference Interpolating Polynomial for the following data:

X	1	2	3	4	5	6
f(x)	12	22	44	84	148	242

Hence, obtain the value of f(x) at x=1.5 and x=2.5. 8

(b) Estimate the missing term (represented by "?") in the following data, if it represents a valid interpolating polynomial of degree 3:

X	1	2	3	4	5
f(x)	5	24	?	128	225

(c) Given the following data for interpolation:

x	0	1	5	15
f(x)	20	60	120	200

To find the value of f(x) at x=2, which of the following methods would you use?
(i) Bessel's interpolation formula
(ii) Newton's Forward Difference Formula
(iii) Lagrange's interpolation method
Give reasons for your answer. 3

(d) What is inverse interpolation? Explain with the help of an example. 3

Attempt any **two** of the following:

5. (a) Find the approximate value of the integral I=$\int_{0.2}^{1.0} \frac{dx}{\sqrt{1+x^2}}$ using Simpson's $\frac{1}{3}$ rule, dividing the interval [0.2,1.0] into four equal sub-intervals. Compute up to four decimal places only. 10

(b) Find the value of f′(x) or y′ and f″(x) or y″ at x=1.25 for the values of y= $x^{2/3}$ given in the following table:

X	1.0	1.5	2.0	2.5	3.0
y =f(x) = $x^{2/3}$	1	1.310	1.587	1.842	2.080

(c) Solve the following differential equation using Euler's method:
y′=1−2xy Assume that y(0)=1.
Find the solution in the interval [0,0.8] with h=0.2. 10

BACHELOR OF COMPUTER APPLICATIONS (BCA) (REVISED)

Chapter 12: Term-End Examination, December- 2019

BCS-054: COMPUTER ORIENTED NUMERICAL TECHNIQUES

Time: 3 Hours
Maximum Marks: 100
Note: 1. Question No. 1 is compulsory. Attempt three more questions from Question No. 2 to 5.
2. Use of any calculator is permitted.

1. (a) Find the absolute error and relative error in the numbers 432.8 and 0.12584 if a four-digit mantissa is used, and chopping is used for approximation. 4

(b) Round the following numbers to two decimal places:

(i) 38.21416
(ii) 4.3742
(iii) 82.375
(iv) 2.4869 2

(c) For the following two floating-point numbers:

x_1=0.5527×10^4
and x_2=0.6243×10^3,

find $x_1 - x_2$. The result should be rounded to four decimal digits. 4

(d) Find the product of x1x_1x1 and x2x_2x2 given in Question 1(c). The result should be chopped to four decimal digits. 3

(e) Find Newton's forward difference interpolating polynomial for the following data and hence obtain the value of f(x) at x=1.5:

x	f(x)
1	34
2	60
3	90
4	124
5	162
6	204

(f) Write the following system of linear equations in matrix form:

x+2y+3z=14
x−y=−1
y+3z=11 2

(g) Solve the following system of linear equations using the Gauss-Seidel iterative method:

x+6y=13
4x−y=2

Perform two iterations, taking x=0 and y=0 as the initial values. 5

(h) Find an interval in which the following equation has a positive root:

$2x^3+x^2-20x+12=0$ 2

(i) Find the forward difference of the following functions for some h>0:

(i) f(x)=3x^2
(ii) f(x)=2x

3

(j) Find the approximate value of the integral I= $\int_0^1 \frac{dx}{1+x^2}$ using the Trapezoidal rule by dividing the interval into five equal parts. 4

2. (a) Using an 8-decimal digit floating-point representation (4 digits for mantissa, 2 for exponent, and 1 each for the sign of the exponent and the sign of the mantissa), represent the following numbers in normalized floating-point form (use chopping if required):

(i) 92752

(ii)−93.231

(iii) −0.0012345 6

(b) Solve the following system of linear equations using the Gaussian elimination method:

$x_1 - x_2 - x_3 = -3$

$2x_1 + 3x_2 + 5x_3 = 7$

$x_1 - 2x_3 + 3x_3 = -11$ 8

(c) Give one example each of the following:

(i) Ill-conditioned problem

(ii) Ordinary differential equation (ODE) of degree 3 and order 2

(iii) A system of inconsistent linear equations in two variables 6

3. (a) Consider the initial-value problem:

y′=0.2xy, y(1)=1

Use Euler's method to obtain an approximation to y(1.2) using h=0.1. 6

(b) Using Lagrange's interpolation formula, find the form of the function y(x) from the following table. Also, compute f(3):

x	y
0	6
2	20
5	56

(c) Write the expressions obtained by applying each of the following operators to f(x) for some h>0:

(i) ∇

(ii) δ

(iii) μ

(iv) E 4

(d) Derive the relation between δ and E. 3

4. (a) Solve the following system of linear equations using partial pivoting:

x+y−5z=0

5x+2y−z=18

2x−2y+z=3 10

(b) Find a real root for the equation

x^3+x−5=0

using the Regula-Falsi method. Perform only two iterations of the method, taking the initial points as x=0 and x=2. 7

(c) Construct Newton's divided difference table for the following data:

x	y
1	10
2	20
4	40
8	80

5. (a) Explain the concept of overflow and underflow in the context of decimal floating-point numbers with the help of one example each. 6

(b) Find the real root of the equation $x^2-3x+1=0$ using Newton-Raphson's method, taking x=2 as the starting value. Show three iterations. 7

(c) Apply Newton's backward difference formula to the data below to obtain a polynomial of degree 4 in x:

x	y
1	1
2	-1
3	1
4	-1
5	1

BACHELOR OF COMPUTER APPLICATIONS (BCA) (REVISED)

Chapter 13: Term-End Examination, June- 2020

BCS-054: COMPUTER ORIENTED NUMERICAL TECHNIQUES

Time: 3 Hours
Maximum Marks: 100
Note: 1. Use of calculator is allowed during the examination.
2. Question No. 1 is compulsory. Attempt any three questions from Question Nos. 2 to 5.

1. (a) Write formulas for absolute error and relative error. If the represented value of is 3.1428 and its actual value is X_1=3.14285, find absolute and relative errors. 4

(b) Solve the following system of linear equations using the Gauss elimination method:

$X_1+X_2+X_3=3$
$4X_1+3X_2+4X_3=11$
$9X_1+3X_2+4X_3=16$ 5

(c) Use the Newton-Raphson method, performing only two iterations, to find a root of the equation x^3−2x−5=0 near the value x=2. 5

(d) Prove that:

Δ=E−1. 3

(e) Using the data given below, find f(2)f(2)f(2) by using Lagrange's interpolation method:

x	f(x)
0	2
1	6
3	8

(f) Calculate the value of the integral $\int_2^3 x^2 dx$ using Simpson's 1/3 rule, taking h=0.2. 6

(g) Given that y′=x^2+y and y(0)=1, determine the value of y when x=0.1, using Euler's method. 6

(h) Assume that a floating point representation is of eight decimal digits with four digits for the normalized mantissa, two digits for the exponent, and one digit each for the sign of the exponent and mantissa. Answer the following using this representation (use chopping if required):

(i) −35678
(ii) +0.0035622
(iii) Addition of numbers given in (i) and (ii) above
(iv) Multiplication of numbers given in (i) and (ii) above. 6

2. (a) Solve the following system of equations using the Gauss-Seidel iteration method. Perform only two iterations, taking x=y=z=0 as the initial approximation:

8x−3y+2z=20
4x+11y−z=33
6x+3y+12z=35 8

(b) Find a root of the equation x^3−2=0 using the Regula-Falsi method. Perform only two iterations. 8

(c) Define the order and degree of a differential equation. Find the order and the degree of the equation:

$$\frac{d^3y}{dx^3} + \left(\frac{dy}{dx}\right)^6 = 0$$ 4

3. (a) Using Newton's forward interpolation formula, obtain the value of y when x=0.4, from the following data:

X	Y
1.1	0.21
1.3	0.69
1.5	1.25
1.7	1.89
1.9	2.61

(b) Evaluate $\int_1^3 \frac{dx}{1+x}$, by subdividing the interval (1,3) into 8 equal parts using the Trapezoidal rule. 6

(c) Solve the following system of equations using the Gauss-Jacobi iteration method. Perform only two iterations:

$8x+y+z=8$

$2x+4y+z=4$

$x+3y+5z=5$ 7

4. (a) Apply Newton's backward difference interpolation formula to find f(x) from the following data. Also, compute f(2.5):

X	f(x)
0	4
2	24
4	39

(b) Solve the following system of linear equations using the Gaussian elimination method with pivotal condensation:

$3x-2y+6z=17$

$6x-y+z=9$

$2x+12y-z=-12$ 10

(c) Explain how the fixed-point method for solving non-linear equations is related to the Newton-Raphson method. 3

5. (a) Evaluate $\int_0^1 e^{-x^2}$ using the Rectangle rule by taking h=0.5. 5

(b) Find the smallest positive root of the equation $x^3-3x-5=0$ using the Bisection method. Perform only three iterations. 6

(c) Write the symbol and formula with respect to f(x) and h for the following operators:

(i) Central difference

(ii) Averaging operator 4

(d) Explain the concept of overflow and underflow in the context of floating point decimal number representation, with the help of one example of each. 5

BACHELOR OF COMPUTER APPLICATIONS (BCA) (REVISED)

Chapter 14: Term-End Examination, February- 2021

BCS-054: COMPUTER ORIENTED NUMERICAL TECHNIQUES

Time: 3 Hours
Maximum Marks: 100
Note: 1. Any calculator is allowed during the examination.
2. Question No. 1 is compulsory. Attempt any three questions from Question Nos. 2 to 5.

1. (a) Define the terms 'accuracy' and 'precision'. If 0.333 is the approximate value of $\frac{1}{3}$, find absolute and relative errors. 4

(b) Solve the following system of equations using the Gauss Elimination method:

x+y+z=3
3x+2y+3z=18
x+4y+9z=16 6

(c) Find the root of the equation x^3+2=0 using Newton-Raphson method, taking initial approximation as −1. Perform only two iterations. 5

(d) Express the operators (i)Δ, (ii), and (iii) δ in terms of operator E. 4

(e) Find the Lagrange interpolating polynomial that fits the following data:

x :	0	1	2
f(x) :	2	3	12

(f) Evaluate the integral $\int_0^6 (x^2 + x + 2)dx$dx using the Trapezoidal rule with h=1.0. 5

(g) Find the smallest positive root of the equation x^2−x−1=0 using the Bisection method. Perform only three iterations. 5

(h) Assume that a floating point representation is of eight decimal digits with four digits for normalized mantissa, two digits for exponent, and one digit each for sign of exponent and mantissa. Answer the following using this representation. Use chopping if required:

(i) 0.035119
(ii)42.169
(iii) Addition of numbers given in (i) and (ii)
(iv) Multiplication of numbers given in (i) and (ii) 5

2. (a) Find the interpolating polynomial fitting the following data using Newton's backward difference interpolating method. 5

x :	0	1	2	3	4
f(x) :	10	9	6	1	-6

(b) Construct the forward difference table and determine the missing term in the following data. You may assume $\Delta^4 y_0$=0:

x:	100	101	102	103	104
f(x):	2.000	2.0043	?	2.0128	2.0170

10

(c) Using the Divided Difference table, verify that for f(x)=x^3, f[a,b,c]=a+b+c. 5

3. (a) Evaluate $\int_1^3 \sqrt{x}\,dx$ using Simpson's $\frac{1}{3}$ rule with h=0.5. 5

(b) Solve the following system of equations using the Gauss-Jacobi method. Perform only two iterations, assuming x_1=x_2=x_3=0 as the initial approximation:

$2x_1-x_2+x_3=-1$

$x_1+2x_2-x_3=6$

$x_1-x_2+2x_3=-3$ 6

(c) Solve the following system of linear equations using the Gaussian elimination method with pivotal condensation:

x+y+10z=14

5x−y+z=9

x−4y+z=−5 9

4. (a) Use the Secant method to find the smallest positive root of the equation f(x)=2^x−5x+2. Perform only two iterations. 7

(b) What are the pitfalls of the Gauss elimination method? Discuss with the help of examples. 5

(c) Given that y′=xy and y(0)=1, determine the value of y when x=0.4, using Euler's method With h=0.1. 8

5. (a) Solve the following system of equations using the Gauss-Seidel method. Perform only two iterations, assuming x_1=x_2=x_3=0 as the initial approximation:

−4x1+x2+10x3=21

5x1−x2+x3=14

2x1+8x2−x3=−7 7

(b) Write the formula for the following operations for a function f(x) and step size h:

(i)Δ

(ii)∇

(iii)δ

(iv)μ

(v)E

(vi)D 6

(c) State the following formulae:

(i) Stirling's formula for interpolation

(ii) Bessel's formula for interpolation 4

(d) Explain the concept of a Boundary Value Problem with a suitable example. 3

BACHELOR OF COMPUTER APPLICATIONS (BCA) (REVISED)

Chapter 15: Term-End Examination, June- 2021

BCS-054: COMPUTER ORIENTED NUMERICAL TECHNIQUES

Time: 3 Hours
Maximum Marks: 100
Note:1. Any calculator is allowed during the examination.
2. Question No. 1 is compulsory. Attempt any three more from the next four questions.

1. (a) Consider the following decimal floating point representation for a number having base 10. Which of the following numbers are not in normalized form? Convert all the numbers to normalized form:

±	d_1	d_2	d_3	d_4	±	e_1	e_2

(i)

+	0	1	2	3	-	1	5

(ii)

-	1	2	3	4	+	0	0

(iii)

-	0	0	0	1	+	0	2

5

(b) Solve the following system of equations using the Gauss-elimination method. Does this method produce a solution for this system?

6x+2y+4z=6
3x+2y+z=3
2x+y+z=0 5

(c) Find the smallest positive root for the equation using the bisection method:

$x^2-6x^2+3=0$

Show three iterations. 7

(d) Construct the difference table for the following data:

x	f(x)
1	6
2	12
3	18
4	25

List the forward differences for f(1) and backward differences for f(4). 3

(e) Write the notation and the formula in terms of f(x)f(x)f(x) and hhh for the following:

(i) Central difference
(ii) Shift operator 2

(f) Find the Newton's forward-difference interpolating polynomial which agrees with the table of values given below:

x	f(x)
1	5
2	14
3	27
4	44
5	65
6	90

Using this polynomial, find the value of f(1.25). 7

(g) Evaluate the integral I= $\int_0^{0.4} \frac{dx}{(1+2x)^2}$ using Simpson's 1/3 rule, by dividing the interval into four equal sub-intervals. 7

(h) Find the order and degree of the following differential equation:

$$5\left(\frac{d^3y}{dx^3}\right)^3 + 12\left(\frac{dy}{dx}\right) - 3x\left(\frac{d^2y}{dx^2}\right)^4 = 0$$ 2

(i) Write the formula for finding the numerical differentiation $\left(\frac{dy}{dx} \text{ and } \frac{d^2y}{dx^2}\right)$. using backward difference formula. 4

2. (a) Perform the following floating point operations (assume the maximum mantissa size to be 4 decimal digits). Use chopping wherever required (answer should be in normalized form):

(i) add 0.2345×10^5 and -0.2205×10^5

(ii) subtract 0.6101×10^1 from 0.2016×10^5

(iii) multiply 0.28× and 0.221×10^4 6

(b) Using the Gauss-Seidel iterative method, solve the following system of linear equations:

2x+y=7

x+4y=14

Use the initial values =0,=1. Perform only two iterations. 6

(c) Using Newton-Raphson method, find the cube root of 10 with initial value as 2. Perform 3 iterations. 8

3. (a) Derive the relationship between EEE and the following operators:

(i)∇

(ii)δ

(iii)μ **6**

(b) Find the value of α in the following data, if f(x) represents a polynomial of degree 3 6

x	**f(x)**
1	**7**
2	**15**
3	***α***
4	**73**
5	**135**

(c) Find Lagrange's interpolating polynomial for the following data:

x	f(x)
1	4
3	18
7	70

Hence evaluate f(4) using the interpolating polynomial. 8

4. (a) The values of y=$x^{1.5}$ are given below for x= 1(1)5. Find the value of y′ and y″ at x=1.5. using Forward Difference (F-D) formula:

x	f(x) : y =$x^{1.5}$
1	1
2	2.8284
3	5.1962
4	8

10

(b) Using Euler's method, solve the differential equation:

y\` = x^3+ y^2,

where y(0)=1.Find the solution on [0, 0.4] with h=0.1. 10

5. (a) Assuming the decimal floating point representation given in Question 1(c), identify what problems will be encountered if you perform the following operations. Explain the problem and propose a solution, if any:

(i) Adding 0.6005×10^{99} with 0.4150×10^{99}

(ii)Adding 0.6705×10^{12}, 0.6685×10^{5} and -0.6705×10^{12}

(iii)Dividing 0.2003×10^{-53} by -0.5000×10^{49} 6

(b) How is truncation error related to Taylor series? Explain with the help of an example. 4

(c) For a given value of hhh, find the values of Δ,Δ^2 and Δ^3 Δ4\Delta^4Δ4, if f(x)=x^2. 5

(d) Derive the formula of the Trapezoidal rule using a diagram. 5

BACHELOR OF COMPUTER APPLICATIONS (BCA) (REVISED)

Chapter 16: Term-End Examination, December- 2021

BCS-054: COMPUTER ORIENTED NUMERICAL TECHNIQUES

Time: 3 Hours
Maximum Marks: 100
Note: 1. Question No. 1 is compulsory. Attempt any three questions from Question Nos. 2 to 5.
2. Any calculator is allowed during the examination.

1. (a) Assuming a four decimal digit mantissa, two-digit exponent, and one digit each for the sign of mantissa and exponent, perform the following arithmetic operations. Indicate overflow, if any. Use chopping if required. The result should be in normalized form.

(i) Add 0.7265×10^{-2} and 0.7105×10^{1}
(ii) Subtract $0.2516\times10^{+2}$ from 0.1001×10^{3}
(iii) Multiply 0.5125×10^{50} and 0.1251×10^{52} 6

(b) Solve the following system of equations using the Gauss-Jacobi iteration method:

5x+2y=19
3x+5y=19

Take the initial estimate as x_0=1 and y_0=1. Perform only two iterations. 5

(c) Write the Newton-Raphson iterative scheme for finding the square root of a positive number n. 4

(d) Write the name and formula of the following operators:

(i) E
(ii) ∇
(iii) δ **3**

(e) Find Newton's forward difference interpolating polynomial for the data given below:

x	1	2	3	4	5	6
y =f(x)	1	12	33	64	105	156

Hence, calculate the value of f(x) at x=1.5. 6

(f) Construct Newton's divided difference table for the following data:

x	**2**	**3**	**5**	**6**
f(x)	**5**	**10**	**26**	**37**

(g) Using Simpson's $\frac{1}{3}rd$ rule, find the approximate value of I= $\int_0^2 \frac{dx}{1+x}$, dividing the interval into four equal sub-intervals. 7

(h) Define the order and degree of a differential equation. What is order and degree of the following differential equation?

$$2\left(\frac{d^4y}{dx^4}\right)^5 + \left(\frac{dy}{dx}\right)^7 + 3x^2\left(\frac{d^2y}{dx^2}\right)^3$$ 3

(i) Write Newton's backward difference formula for evaluating $\frac{dy}{dx}$. 2

2. (a) Solve the following equations using the Gaussian elimination method with row interchange/pivotal condensation method:

y+z=1
2x+3y+4z=4
4x+2y−3z=11 8

(b) Find the first positive root of the equation $x^3+x^2-10=0$ by the Regula-Falsi method. Show two iterations. 7

(c) Find the Taylor/Maclaurin series for f(x)=e^x around x=0. 5

3. (a) Represent the following operators in terms of EEE:
(i)Δ
(ii)∇
(iii) δ 3

(b) Find the missing term (?) in the following data, where f(x) is a polynomial of degree 3:

x	1	2	3	4	5
f(x)	-3	10	?	78	145

Also, find the interpolating polynomial using the backward difference. 10

(c) Find the interpolating polynomial that fits the following data:

x	1	2	5
f(x)	4	7	28

using Lagrange's interpolating polynomial method. 7

4. (a) Given the following values of x and f(x) for x=1$(0.5)^3$:

x	1	1.5	2	2.5	3
y = f(x)	2	4.875	10	18.125	30

Find y′ and y″ at x=1.25 using the Forward Difference (FD) formula. 10

(b) Use Euler's method to find the solution of the differential equation
y\` =t^4+y^3 given that,y(0)=1
Find the solution in the interval [0,0.9] with h=0.3. 10

5. (a) Explain the formula for the Trapezoidal rule with the help of a diagram. Also, find the approximate value of I= $\int_0^1 \frac{dx}{1+x}$ using the Trapezoidal rule with only one interval. 5

(b) What is Inverse Interpolation? Explain with the help of an example. 4

(c) Explain whether, in arithmetic with 4 significant digits, the problem of solving the following system of linear equations is ill-conditioned or not:
(2.0000)x+(0.6667)y=2.0000
(1.0000)x+(0.3333)y=1.0000 5

(d) Compare and contrast the following methods:
(i) Gauss elimination method and Gauss-Seidel iterative method
(ii) Bisection method and Regula-Falsi method 6

BACHELOR OF COMPUTER APPLICATIONS (BCA) (REVISED)

Chapter 17: Term-End Examination, June- 2022

BCS-054: COMPUTER ORIENTED NUMERICAL TECHNIQUES

Time: 3 Hours
Maximum Marks: 100
Note:1. Any calculator is allowed during the examination.
2. Question No. 1 is compulsory. Attempt any three more from the next four questions.

1. (a) Solve the following system of equations using Gauss Elimination method:

$x+2y+z=3$
$2x+3y+3z=10$
$3x-y+2z=13$ 6

(b) Perform two iterations using the Gauss-Seidel iteration method to solve the following system of equations:

$10x-2y-z-w=3$
$-2x+10y-z-w=15$
$-x-y+10z-2w=27$
$-x-y-2z+10w=-9$ 6

(c) Find the root of the equation $x^3-x-1=0$ lying between 1 and 2 by using the Bisection method (perform three iterations). 6

(d) Verify the relation $\Delta-\nabla = \Delta\nabla$, where Δ and $\nabla$are forward and backward differencing operations, respectively. 6

(e) Write Stirling's formula of numerical differentiation. Briefly discuss its application with a suitable example. 6

(f) Find f(5) by Lagrange's interpolation method for the following data:

x	f(x)
1	0
3	8
4	48
6	180
10	900

5

(g) Compute the integral of function f(x) using the Trapezoidal rule. The values of f(x) for values of x between 0 and 1 are tabulated below:

x	f(x)
0	1
0.1	1.2
0.2	1.4
0.3	1.6
0.4	1.8
0.5	2.0

2. (a) Perform the following conversions:

(i) $(-349)_0$ to its binary equivalent.

(ii) $(-0.3125)_{10}$ to its binary equivalent. 6

(b) Compare direct methods and iterative methods of solving linear algebraic equations. Give merits and demerits of each. Provide one method for each category (direct and iterative). 6

(c) Explain Newton-Raphson's iterative method for finding the qth root of a positive number N. Also, find the cube root of 10 correct to three decimal places, taking the initial estimate as 2.0. 8

3. (a) Verify the following:

(i) Δf(x)=0 when f(x)=c, a constant

(ii) Δ^2f(x)=0 when f(x)=x, an identity function

(iii) $E^2x^2 = x^2$ +8x+16when x varies by a constant increment of 2 6

(b) Construct a difference table for the data given below:

X	f(x)
1	7
2	13
3	18
4	25

Perform the following:

(i) Highlight the forward differences for f(1)

(ii) Highlight the backward differences for f(4)

(iii) Find the highest degree of polynomial that can be generated 7

(c) Write short notes on the following in the context of floating-point representation:

(i) Precision

(ii) Accuracy

(iii) Significant digits

Give a suitable example for each. 7

4. (a) If f(x)=x^3, find the first and second divided differences for x={a,b,c}. 5

(b) Evaluate the integral I= $\int_0^{0.8} \frac{dx}{\sqrt{1+x}}$ using Simpson's 1/3 rule, dividing the interval 0 to 0.8 to 4 equal subintervals. (Compute up to five decimal places). 5

(c) Use the modified Euler method to find the value of y for x=0.1 and x=0.2 from the differential equation $\frac{dy}{dx} = x^2+y^2 - 2$, y (0)=1. 1

(Compute up to five decimal places). 10

5. (a) Using the Runge-Kutta method of order 4, obtain yyy when x=1.1, given that y=1.2 when x=1, and y satisfies the equation $\frac{dy}{dx}$= 3x+y^2 10

(b) Write the formula for Euler's method and use it to find the solution of the equation y'= f(t+y) = t+y, given by, y(0)=1 1

Find the solution on the interval [0,0.8] with step size h=0.2. 10

BACHELOR OF COMPUTER APPLICATIONS (BCA) (REVISED)

Chapter 18: Term-End Examination, December- 2022

BCS-054: COMPUTER ORIENTED NUMERICAL TECHNIQUES

Time: 3 Hours
Maximum Marks: 100
Note:1. Any calculator is allowed during the examination.
2. Question No. 1 is compulsory. Attempt any three more from the next four questions.

1. (a) Solve the following system of equations using the Gauss Elimination method:

$$2x_1 + 8x_2 + 2x_3 = 14$$
$$x_1 + 6x_2 - x_3 = 13$$
$$2x_1 - x_2 + 2x_3 = 5$$

6

(b) Solve the following system of equations by using the Gauss-Seidel iteration method (perform two iterations):

8x−3y+2z=20
6x+3y+12z=35
4x+11y−z=33

6

(c) Determine the value of $\sqrt{12}$ by the Newton-Raphson method (perform 3 iterations), taking =3.5 as the initial estimate. 6

(d) Verify the relation (1+Δ)(1−∇)=1, where Δ and ∇ are forward and backward differencing operators, respectively. 6

(e) Write Bessel's formula of numerical differentiation. Briefly discuss its application with a suitable example. 6

(f) Using Lagrange's interpolation method, find the interpolating polynomial that fits the data given below:

x_k	f_k
0	**2**
1	**3**
2	**12**
5	**147**

(g) Write Simpson's $\frac{1}{3}$ rule and use it to compute the integral of the function f(x), with the respective values of xxx and f(x) given below: 6

x	f(x)
0	1
0.1	1.01
0.2	1.04
0.3	1.09
0.4	1.16
0.5	1.25
0.6	1.36
0.7	1.49
0.8	1.64
0.9	1.81
1.0	2.0

2. (a) Briefly discuss the terms accuracy, precision, and significant digits with suitable examples of each. 6

(b) Write the formula for the Gauss-Jacobi iterative method. Solve the following system of equations using the Gauss-Jacobi method (perform three iterations):

$$-4x_1 + x_2 + 10x_3 = 21$$
$$5x_1 - x_2 + x_3 = 14$$
$$2x_1 + 8x_2 - x_3 = -7$$

7

(c) Write the formula for the Secant method. Use it to perform three iterations for finding roots of the equation $x^3+4x^2-10=0$ near x=0 and x=1. (compute up to two decimal places only). 7

3. (a) Verify the following:

(i) Δ^3f(x)=0, when f(x)=x^2

(ii) E^nf(x)= e^{x+nh}, where f(x)=x^2 6

(b) Find the Newton's forward difference interpolating polynomial which agrees with the following data:

x	f(x)
1	10
2	19
3	40
4	79
5	142
6	235

Also, obtain the value of f(x) at x=1.5. 7

(c) Find the Lagrange's interpolating polynomial for the following data:

x	f(x)
$\frac{1}{4}$	-1
$\frac{1}{3}$	2
1	7

4. (a) If $f(x)=\frac{1}{x}$, show that: $f(a,b,c)=\frac{+1}{abc}$ using the divided difference table for x={a,b,c}. 5

(b) Evaluate the integral $I=\int_0^1 \frac{dx}{\sqrt{1+x^2}}$ using the Trapezoidal rule, dividing the interval [0,1] into 5 equal parts (compute up to 5 decimal places only). 5

(c) Use Euler's method to find the solution of the IVP: $y'=-2t,, y(0)=1$ Take the interval [0,1] with a step size h=0.2. 10

5. (a) Using the Runge-Kutta method of order 4, approximate y when x=0.1 and x=0.2, given that x=0 when y=1 and $\frac{dy}{dx}=x+y$ (Take h=0.1). 10

(b) Differentiate between the following:

(i) Euler's method and modified/improved Euler's method

(ii) Runge-Kutta method (order 2) and Runge-Kutta method (order 4)

Give advantage and disadvantage of each 10

BACHELOR OF COMPUTER APPLICATIONS (BCA) (REVISED)

Chapter 19: Term-End Examination, June- 2023

BCS-054: COMPUTER ORIENTED NUMERICAL TECHNIQUES

Time: 3 Hours
Maximum Marks: 100
Note: 1. Any calculator is allowed during the examination.
2. Question No. 1 is compulsory. Attempt any three more from the next four questions.

1. (a) Use Gauss elimination method to solve the following system of linear equations:

$$x_1 + x_2 + x_3 = 3$$
$$4x_1 + 3x_2 + 4x_3 = 8$$
$$9x_1 + 3x_2 + 4x_3 = 7$$ 6

(b) Use the Gauss Jacobi method to solve the following system of linear equations (results should be correct up to two decimal places):

$$-4x_1 + x_2 + 10x_3 = 21$$
$$5x_1 - x_2 + x_3 = 14$$
$$2x_1 + 8x_2 - x_3 = -7$$ 6

(c) Use the Bisection method to find the positive root of the equation:
$x^3 + 4x^2 - 10 = 0$ correct to two decimal places. 6

(d) Perform the following:
(i) Express operator E in terms of operator δ.
(ii) Express operator μ in terms of operator δ. 6

(e) Determine the Newton's forward difference interpolating polynomial that satisfies the following data:

x	f(x)
1	1
2	4
3	9
4	16
5	25

Also, find the value of f(x) at x=1.7. 6

(f) Determine y′ and 'y″ at x=2.25 using Newton's Forward Difference (FD) formula for the following data:

x	$y = \sqrt{x}$
1.5	**1.2247**
2.0	**1.4142**
2.5	**1.5811**
3.0	**1.7320**
3.5	**1.8708**

(g) Calculate the value of the integral $\int_4^{5.2} \log(x)dx$,using the Trapezoidal rule (assume h=0.2). 5

2. (a) Use Euler's method to find the solution of y′= f(t+y) = t+y, given that y(0)=1. Take h=0.2 and find the solution on [0,0.8]. 8

(b) Find the Maclaurin series for f(x)=e^x around x=0. 4

(c) Determine the approximate root of the equation:

$$\cos x - xe^{x} = 0$$

using the Secant method with initial approximations x_0=0 and x_1=1. Perform two iterations. 8

3. (a) Write the Newton-Raphson iterative scheme to find the inverse of an integer N. Hence, find the inverse of 17 correct up to 4 decimal places, starting with 0.05. 8

(b) Write expressions for Δ, ∇ , δ, and μ operators in terms of operator E. 4

(c) Find Lagrange's interpolating polynomial for the following data:

X	f(x)
$\frac{1}{4}$	-1
$\frac{1}{3}$	2
1	7

4. (a) Use a Divided Difference table to find the value of f(a,b,c) for f(x)=x^3. 4

(b) Use Stirling's formula for differentiation on the following data to find the value of x for which f(x) attains its maximum value:

X	y = f(x)
1	7
2	15
3	21
4	19
5	3

(c) Evaluate $\int_0^1 \frac{dx}{(1+2x)^2}$ using Simpson's rule. Subdivide the interval [0,1] into 6 equal parts. 6

5. (a) Solve the Initial Value Problem (IVP) y′= -ty^2 , y(2)=1 and find y(2.1) and y(2.2). using the modified Euler's method with h=0.1. 10

(b) Use the classical Runge-Kutta method of order 4 to solve the IVP y′=2y+3e^t, y(0)=0; and find y(0.1),y(0.2), and y(0.3). 10

9 789369 722105

Printed at Repro India Ltd.